# I Love You Dad!

## A personalized I love you to the best father in the world:

_____

*put a picture of yourself here*

**By** _____

**Date:** _____

Fathers are one in a million.

They form a special bond with their children that lasts a lifetime. They are the ones who guide their children. They keep them safe when needed and help build a strong foundation.

Simply put...fathers are marvelous. This book is dedicated to all fathers and is a testimony to one special father. This book was written by a child that believes **you** are a special dad! Know that if you are getting this book, someone thinks you are truly one in a billion.

Thanks Dad!

# Outback Books

Summary: Here's why I have the best
father in the world.

Author:
Ideas by: Christopher Forest
Editor: Melissa Forest

ISBN: 978-1503309678

Outbook Books
A division of Outhouse Books
Danvers, MA  01923
1 2 3 4 5 6 7 8 9 0 1
© 2014

THANK YOU DAD. YOU TRULY ARE
AMAZING!!! THIS BOOK IS FOR YOU.

# Dedication page

This book is dedicated to my father. I wrote this book for him for many reasons. Here is what I want him to know.

_____

_____

_____

_____

_____

_____

_____

I love you Dad.

Love,

_____

A Picture of My Father

Dad, I love you. Here are three reasons why!

1. _____

   _____

   _____

2. _____

   _____

   _____

3. _____

   _____

   _____

# Questions I Always Wanted to Ask My Father

_____

_____

_____

_____

_____

_____

_____

_____

_____

# MY FATHER ACROSTIC

*Complete this acrostic for your father. Write a word or phrase for each letter.*

**M**

**Y**

**F**

**A**

**T**

**H**

**E**

**R**

# Quotes about fathers

"My father gave me the greatest gift anyone could give another person; he believed in me."
- Jim Valvano

"I cannot think of any need in childhood as strong as the need for a father's protection."
- Sigmund Freud

"A father carries pictures where his money used to be."
- Anonymous

"One father is more than a hundred schoolmasters."
- George Herbert

"Father! To God himself we could not give a holier name."
- William Wordsworth

Here is a picture of my favorite memory
with my father.

The best place I have ever been with my

father is _____.


When I was there, what I remember most is

_____

_____

_____

_____

_____

_____

_____

**When I think of Dad, I think of** *(fill the page with as many words as you can think).*

# My definition of a father

Father: _____

_____

_____

_____

_____

_____

Complete these sentences about your father

1. When I think of my father, I think

he is _____.

2. My father is as smart as a(n)

_____.

3. I always have fun with my father

because he is _____

_____.

# Three ways Dad makes me feel special!

# WORD SEARCH

*Make a word search for your father. Think of words that remind you of him and hide them in this word search. List the words below for your father to find.*

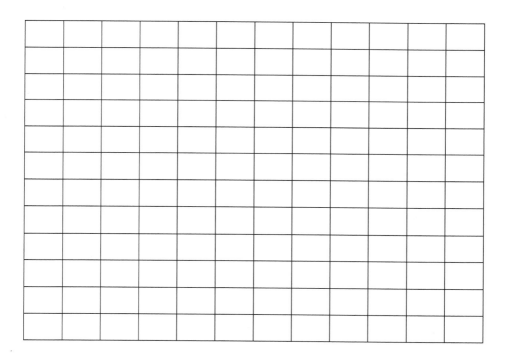

## Words to look for:

# Famous Fathers:

Father Time – he is in charge of the changing year

Father Goose – Cary Grant character who served as a plane spotter in the Pacific during World War II

Father of his country – nickname given to the first president, George Washington

Father Serra – a Franciscan friar who helped establish missions in California

Father of Medicine – the nickname of Hippocrates

Father of the Bride – character in two separate movie series, played by Spencer Tracy and (in the remake) by Steve Martin

Three things I like to do with my father.

1.

2.

3.

Play games with your father on this page,
like tic-tac-toe.

# One lesson my father taught me is:

_____

_____

_____

_____

_____

_____

_____

_____

# Words of advice from my Dad!

My special name for my Dad is:

_____

I like this name because:

_____

_____

_____

_____

# Four reasons I am thankful for my father

1. _____

_____

2. _____

_____

3. _____

_____

4. _____

_____

# My recipe for the best father

Ingredients:

Directions:

_____

_____

_____

_____

_____

# Things I want to do with my father

_____     _____

_____     _____

_____     _____

_____     _____

_____     _____

_____     _____

_____     _____

_____     _____

Someday, if I am lucky to be a parent like
my Dad, here is what I would be like:

_____

_____

_____

_____

_____

_____

# A Letter to my Father

Date: _____

Dear _____

_____

_____

_____

_____

_____

_____

_____

_____

I love you Dad

Here's a picture of a special hug I have for you *(make sure to hug the picture at the end so it is captured forever.)*

# Timeline of my father and me

_____

_____

_____

_____

_____

_____

_____

_____

_____

# My memory page for father:

My name: _____

My age: _____

Today's date: _____

Games I play with my father: _____

_____

My first memory of Dad: _____

_____

How I like to spend time with my

father:_____

_____

# World's Best Father Award

Given to:_____

To my father, who is kind, intelligent, strong, loyal, brave, clever, hard-working, and helpful. For meritorious service as a father, going above and beyond his duties.

By: _____

Awarded on (date): _____

Made in United States
Orlando, FL
13 June 2025

62092059R00020